Stronger

Stronger
(What Doesn't Kill You)

An Addict's Mom's Guide to Peace

SANDY L. SHERMAN

NEW YORK

NASHVILLE • MELBOURNE • VANCOUVER

Stronger
(What Doesn't Kill You)
An Addict's Mom's Guide to Peace

Published in New York, New York, by Morgan James Publishing in partnership with Difference Press. Morgan James is a trademark of Morgan James, LLC. www.MorganJamesPublishing.com

The Morgan James Speakers Group can bring authors to your live event. For more information or to book an event visit The Morgan James Speakers Group at www.TheMorganJamesSpeakersGroup.com.

ISBN 978-1-68350-478-8 paperback
ISBN 978-1-68350-479-5 eBook
Library of Congress Control Number: 2017902779

Editing: Cynthia Kane

Author's photo courtesy of Kim Jew Photography Studios

Cover Design by:
Rachel Lopez
www.r2cdesign.com

Interior Design by:
Bonnie Bushman
The Whole Caboodle Graphic Design

Dedication

To all the Mothers of Addicted Kids who have the courage to take their lives back

To Bob, my wonderful husband. Thank you for believing in me and supporting me throughout this process and being my biggest fan!

To Andrew & Alexis, my most valuable teachers

To my animals, my horses: Cody, Amondo, TG, Glorietta, Shammy, Mojo, Dew and Richard, my dogs: Keagan, Dusty, Brandi, Sampson, Kita and Merlin, thank you for always being there for me, for helping me heal, for bringing me your love and affection no matter what.

Table of Contents

Foreword

This book is a no nonsense, unorthodox method to taking your life back and reclaiming your power as a mother of an addict. This book is Sandy's journey of being an addict's mom where she has overcome incredible challenges in her life dealing with her son and daughter's drug and alcohol addiction.

Sandy shares her journey to where her own evolvement is what saved her own life and that of her family by letting her kids go to make their own decisions about their lives and to take 100% responsibility for their decisions. As Sandy stepped back, she began to learn valuable lessons and ask herself very powerful questions like "Did I cause this?", "Was I responsible for my kids choices?". She began her healing journey when she truthfully and sometime painfully answered the questions. When the realization came to her that it wasn't her fault, she began to take action in healing by dealing with the fear, anger, helplessness and desperation head on. Sandy shares her method of reclaiming her life through recovery of her own life with you in this book.

The issue of addiction is very real in many families. The shame and guilt felt by the mothers, parents and other family members is almost incomprehensible. It's time that you take a stand and fight this fight, but from a position of strength, not weakness. It's an empowering force to transfer the responsibility back to your kids and stop taking the blame for their addiction. Once you do, you will find that you can and will help them through this, but with a mindset of helping vs. enabling.

It's all here. All you need to know about taking your life back, finding the strength, love and patience to create positive, everlasting change, finally letting go and reclaim your power is right here. Some of the questions in this book are:

- Do I blame myself for my kids' addiction?
- Do my kids blame me for their lives and the decisions that they have made?

- Did I raise my kids to be addicts?
- What do I uniquely offer this world?
- What am I grateful for today?

How not to lose sight of what's important. It is an investment in yourself and your family. You matter and you will realize that addiction affects many, not just the addict. Sandy so eloquently explains that forgiveness of yourself plays a huge part of the healing process and to begin setting boundaries.

In this book, you will find the exact method that Sandy used to aid in her recovery from enabling her kids and trying to save them to forgiving herself and taking responsibility for her own life. There are steps, keys and affirmations throughout the book, which will help you begin your recovery and take your life back. The stories are real and heartfelt and you will find yourself resonating with them. I applaud her for being so utterly honest and putting herself out there for the world to see and how she recovered. Sandy's purpose for writing this book is to help mothers find peace and to believe in themselves enough to handle an addiction in their family.

Stronger (What doesn't kill you) is a book about the recovery of the mother/parent. It's a book about you, about your journey, about your healing and recovery. It's about giving yourself permission to be happy. It's about letting go of the resistance, the fear and the anger and finally emerge into the person you were meant to be. It's about setting yourself free of the blame and responsibility and of being the victim. It's about becoming strong enough to handle your life so you can handle theirs.

If you want to change, if you are ready to change, then this book will inspire you to change your circumstances, allow yourself to envision a life where you have clarity, peace, strength and happiness.

—JB Glossinger,
Founder MorningCoach.com CEO,
Alive Foundation Inc

Introduction

Being an Addicts' Mom is one of the most heart wrenching places to be in life. You constantly question yourself. Did you do everything possible to prevent your child from using? Did you spend enough time with them? Did you influence them in a good way? Did you not pay attention to them when they needed you the most?

I blamed myself for my daughter's addiction. I was in constant denial and made excuses for her all of the time when questioned by family on how she was doing. I would lie for her and I would make light of her future that she just didn't know what she wanted to do with her life.

This book is the tale of my journey and how I took my life back and reclaimed my power. After many years of trying to talk to her, reason with her, get angry and hysterical at her, I had enough. She would not stop! This drug had a hold of her so much so that she began to lie, cheat and steal just to get another fix. She stole from us, everything from forging checks, to stealing all my Jewelry, Dvd's, Cd's, Camera's, iPods, etc., anything of value that she could sell. The worst thing she stole and sold for drugs was our guns: 3 rifles and 5 handguns running approximately $8000. Even when we discovered them missing, I still believed her when she said she didn't do it.

I wanted so much to be a part of my daughter's life, but something else took her over, it was her addiction. It had a hold of her so hard, that it had replaced me as Mom in her life. I couldn't get over the fact that when I would look at her she could hardly open her eyes or hold a conversation. She wore long sleeves all of the time to hide the needle marks. And, when she could not find a vein any longer because her veins had collapsed, she started shooting up in her hands and between her toes. Why was she doing this to herself? Her drug of choice was Heroin. It was the devil in disguise for sure and he had taken my daughter from me and I will never forget him or forgive him. He had destroyed my family and I didn't know how to get it back.

My purpose is to help other mothers that are in the same situation. Our kids are killing us in ways that are unimaginable, through our thoughts and their actions. What we need to do though, to handle the situation, to gain some sense of peace, is to believe in ourselves. Ask ourselves questions like: Did I cause this? Did I put the needle in my daughter's arm? Am I responsible for her choices and decisions? Did I influence her life in such a way that she would harm her body for a drug? The answer? NO. I realized I didn't do any of those things. My daughter did. What I had to do was turn my thinking around. Transfer the responsibility from myself to my daughter where it belonged. Everything she did, she made a conscience choice to do so, by her own volition. I did not tie her arms behind her back and make her do this.

When I realized this, I began to take action. I cut off her funds, no more money when she asked or begged for it. Her friends were not allowed over, because they were just as bad, if not worse, than she was and they all were in so deep with drug addiction. No more letting her drive my car, she had wrecked her car once, which we paid to have fixed and then she wrecked it again. It sat in the garage for a year and we finally sold it for scrap.

I started reading everything on personal growth, inner work and development of my own mind and soul. I educated myself on addiction so I had tools to offer both my kids, if they wanted to change their lives. It was liberating to think that there was nothing wrong with me outside of the normal shit that we think about ourselves.

The Mothers that have loved their kids unconditionally are the ones hit the worst by this addiction. They truly love their child. They gave birth to them, changed their diapers, fed them, took them to their first day of school, watched them play sports, go to school, have birthday parties, watched them in band, and fed all their friends pizza to celebrate something. That's why it's so damn hard to accept that their precious child that they love with all their heart is a drug addict or an alcoholic. If you're this mother let me tell you it's going to be okay. I want you to realize you can reclaim your power and take your life back, realizing that your child's choices are not yours.

Why are we as parents so reluctant to let our child go? Because we fear that we'll never see them again. We fear them living on the streets, hot in the summer, cold in the winter with no shelter. After all, this is our child and we want to protect them. We fear prostitution, attacks and/or rape, not knowing what they are doing, and being left behind.

This book is about finding that positive change that you need to live your life as you deserve to live it. Free of guilt, shame, helplessness and fear. Throughout the book you will find reflective and powerful questions to ask yourself, along with affirmations and exercises. There are tools and keys for you to find that positive change you are looking for. If you are ready to take action, to take your life back, to find the peace you are looking for, then this book is for you.

This book is NOT about making excuses, staying stuck and passing the responsibility of your child's addiction onto yourself. If you are not ready, please read no further. It's an eye opener, for sure, when we realize we have no one but ourselves to heal. It's an unorthodox method of healing the Mother of the Addict and not the addict themselves. Are you ready to make a change?

Then I invite you to read on....

Part 1

The Love of a Mother

Chapter 1

The Awakening

"I have loved you with an everlasting love."
—(Jeremiah 31:3)

My Story

We pulled in the parking lot of the rehab center on a Monday afternoon in April 2012. It was a residential recovery center that was recommended to us by a family member whose daughter had resided there 10 years earlier. It was in Phoenix, Arizona and I remember thinking how unusually hot it was for April at 100 degrees. As we sat there looking at all of these cute cottages, I thought, "it's not going to be that bad" I felt a little relief. After an exhausting 7-hour drive, I helped my daughter collect her bags and belongings. She got out of the car and was still wrapped in her blanket and carrying her pillow from home. "It's 100 degrees Lex, take off that blanket." But she was feeling unusually cold. Everything was labeled with her name on it and I had to do some special shopping as the Center's requirements for shampoo, deodorant, and soap to be alcohol free. We walked in as a family, Bob, Lexi and myself. The house was furnished with comfortable couches, chairs, full kitchen, dining room and 2 bathrooms, a big screen TV, all the comforts of home. When we walked in, all the girls turned and looked at us and just seemed to stare. This center was for women only, which was another relief to me, no distractions. Every woman in the living room was a recovering drug addict or alcoholic and I suddenly became extremely uncomfortable. I prayed that Lexi would fit in with these women and I became frightened for her.

A woman came out of the office and greeted us and then turned to Lexi and told her to dump all of her belongings onto the living room floor for inspection. I thought that was weird, and a little unnerving, but they had to do that for her safety and the safety of the residents. Then another woman asked to talk with Lexi privately and they went outside for about 10 minutes while her Dad and I finished up paperwork and intake. By this time, I was on the verge of tears, as I knew that when we finished intake, we had to leave and say goodbye to our daughter for 5 months. I was scared for her and I was scared for me. When it was time to say goodbye, I stood and really looked at my daughter, she had lost so much weight, she was down to 85lbs. I reached out to hug her and cried uncontrollably and I could see in her eyes that she was not okay with this. I had never felt so much love for my baby girl as I did in that moment. But, I knew in my soul of souls, she had to be there. I knew we had to save her life because she wasn't going to make that decision for herself. She liked being an addict, high on Heroin for 5 years, she liked the way it made her feel, she didn't have to face reality or responsibility. She didn't have to feel anything. During the drive, she shot up every time we stopped to take a break. It was her last hurrah I suppose, but it would be that much more painful when she went through withdrawal. What I didn't admit to myself was that she had no intention of staying clean; she was just going to bide her time.

My son, Andrew, is also an addict. He's been an alcoholic for the past 12 years, on and off in rehab and detox centers and many attempts to quit drinking on his own, at home, in front of his Wife and Son.

Addiction had taken over my kids, they were no longer mine to claim because a bigger, more persuasive demon had possessed them and convinced them that they no longer needed anything else in life, not even their Mother. The addiction was in full control and there was nothing I could do about it, but I fought back long and hard. With Lexi, I didn't know what to do or where to turn and I kept our dirty little secret to myself for as long as I could. For the 3 years prior to knowing about the addiction, I led my life as a normal Mom and Wife and everything was good. I had no clue to what my Daughter was doing under our own roof. It didn't occur to me that my daughter could be a drug addict. There were tell tale signs and clues; I didn't see it coming or I chose to ignore it. Most likely the latter. The biggest mistake I made was not being aware of the clues, things started to turn up missing, DVD's, CD's, jewelry, including my measuring spoons. I second-guessed myself all along and just thought I was becoming absent minded and had misplaced these items.

I would ask my husband if he lent out any movies or CD's because I couldn't find this one or that one. But, I shrugged it off and went about my life. I was in total denial.

During the 2 years before rehab I was noticing that my daughter was becoming more distant and reclusive and would sleep an enormous amount of time, usually part or all of the day only to get up when she had to use the bathroom. Sleep all day and out all night. I couldn't even stomach her room as it was filled with a rancid smell of who knows what. Dirty clothes all over the place, half eaten something or other on her nightstand. Her dog slept in her room and used it as her personal little campground because Lexi would not take her outside to do her business. I was absolutely disgusted and sick to my stomach most days. Her room was a different world, one that I wasn't used to. My house was spotlessly clean outside of her room. When I did need to go in there, I would knock and then enter cautiously and would find her dead to the world sleeping with her mouth open. It was really difficult to wake her, but when she managed to half way open her eyes, she couldn't understand what I was saying to her. So, I would just leave her room and close the door. I didn't even know her anymore.

Life As We Know it to be True and The Lies We Live By
It was like a ticking time bomb that I knew would blow up in our faces. The person I was becoming was something out of a horror film. I was so angry. I was obsessed with finding out what my daughter was on that I waited until she would leave the house so I could make a beeline into her room to search it. It wasn't a calm search; it was a hysterical, fanatical "I'm going to find drugs in this room or something that would prove my suspicions" kind of search. I turned over her mattress, I tore her closet apart, I turned her dresser drawers upside down; I looked inside her shoes. Who am I? Some kind of freak that was absolutely out of control. I needed to know and I needed to know now. I found nothing. She took the drugs and all of the paraphernalia with her in her backpack. She was smarter than me and getting smarter by the day. She told me what I wanted to hear.

My life at this point was filled with stress and anger and a lot of fear. I was beside myself with doubt, but my gut told me that I was on the right track, but how was I going to prove it? I didn't know. I tried to maintain calmness on the outside so no one would notice that my stomach was churning and I was constantly preoccupied. I had a company to run, but my mind was never there. I had no idea what I was doing from moment to moment. I just knew that my baby girl was in trouble. I would try and talk to her mother to daughter, but she wouldn't be honest with me and would just tell me that I was imagining things. She didn't want to give up her life with Heroin, so she would lie to my face as she was about to score another bag from her dealer. I told myself lies to make myself feel better and to get me through the day. Lies like, I believe her, it would never be my daughter, she wouldn't do that to me, she's a good girl, etc. I didn't know what to believe anymore. All the time and effort I took to try to reason with her and to let her know if she needed help I was there had fallen on deaf ears. She didn't want my help; she just wanted to be left alone to do her drugs, in my house, and nothing else. I knew I needed to change my way of dealing with the situation. And while I'd spent so much time wanting and trying to help my daughter who didn't want it, I realized it was me who wanted and needed help. I needed to step back and start to take care of myself.

Bending, Manipulation and Denial

I was a denial queen for so long before I realized that being in that state did not help my daughter. What it did was give her continued permission to use. The state of mind I was in prior to realizing that I needed to do something about it was I just didn't want to believe it. It just wasn't true, or was it? Maybe it would go away. How ridiculous this sounds now. As a parent, we must first admit that there is a problem and go to great lengths to solve it. How do you solve it? You admit that they are using and you step into the truth. You take a stand now and you stop them from manipulating and lying to your face. Once we do this then we are getting somewhere!

It's a Family Disease

I have heard and read this so much while my kids were using. I got so sick and tired about hearing that substance abuse was a disease. I used to think that, wait a minute, they didn't walk down an alley and catch drug abuse or alcoholism! How ignorant I really was in the beginning. There are at least 4 people affected by the addiction in your family, at least 4!! It's astounding to me! You as the Parent are very much emotionally part of the addiction, if not more so, than the child. They use because it numbs their feelings and they continue because it works! But, you as the Mom with your wits about you and nothing to numb your feelings, know that your family has been through hell. It takes a village of support to get through this. I just want to say that you matter and it's not your fault. Educate yourself on their drug of choice. Do your research on what the drugs do to their bodies, what the symptoms are, and signs to look for. When the drug abuse became apparent for me, it became my mission to do my research on signs, symptoms, withdrawals, and recovery. I wanted and needed to know the effects the drugs were having on my daughter's body and mind so I would be in a better position to help her and to finally realize that the drug was now necessary and not a choice.

What is an Addict and This is Not My Child!

I finally figured out that there is no way to have a normal relationship with an addict. I tried, but sadly failed. I would bribe them, enable them, tried to treat them as if we were some big happy family. At first, I didn't understand the chemical effects that addiction had on my kids. It starts as a choice and then becomes a necessity. They cannot live without it and it's an uncontrollable need to satisfy a hunger we, as parents, do not understand. The substance turns our kids into something other than our kids. They become raving maniacs at the drop of the hat, you ask them a question and if it rubs them wrong, they turn into their Jekyll and Hyde version of a horror movie and you wonder where that came from. The addiction causes them to be people that steal, lie, cheat and do unthinkable things to get their drugs or alcohol. They have no consideration for anyone or anything but themselves. They make promises they have no intention of keeping just to manipulate you into doing or giving them what they want. Been there, done that.

My wonderful husband is a gun collector. We have a Winchester safe in our bedroom that is double and triple locked and has a combination. Since we have no little kids in our house, he never locked it, just shut it and closed the latch. He suggested we go to the shooting range to shoot the new gun he bought me. I'm not an advocate of guns, but he is trying to teach me gun safety and loves me enough to teach me how to shoot. So, I agreed, let's go. He opened his safe to choose a couple of rifles and a couple of handguns, one of which he bought me. I was kind of excited that we could do something together, even if it was going to the shooting range. He started pulling out the boxes where the guns were stored in their original packages and they were all empty. There were 5 handguns missing and 3 rifles missing, gone! We looked at each other; we were in shock! Where did they go? Oh my God! After he collected himself, he started looking in his safe for the valuables we kept in there; things like my diamond wedding ring (I wear a band, so I put my ring in the safe), several other rings, necklaces, gold coins, etc., they were all gone. He looked at me and said "Go get Alexis". I went to her room and got her out of bed. She could barely walk and when she stumbled into our room wrapped in a blanket that I don't think had been washed in a year she stood there and wondered what we wanted. Her Dad asked her about the guns and she didn't know anything. She denied everything and said she didn't know what we were talking about. I confronted her and again she said she didn't know anything. Fast forward 2 months, after we both turned into raving hysterical maniacs threatening her very life if she didn't tell the truth, she finally admitted that she was talked into taking the guns and selling them to the dealer for Heroin by a drug buddy. They were worth combined about $10,000. Along with the guns, my wedding ring and all my jewelry was gone, sold for bottom dollar at the nearest pawnshop. What's so bizarre is that I believed her at first! Here's my denial pouring in, I would rationalize to myself and my husband, why would she take the guns? What would she do with them? My poor husband threatened to call the police and I talked him out of it to protect my daughter. A month later, I felt that there was justice and that God heard my cries for help. She had a car accident, she rear-ended a couple making a left turn and it was in front of the police station. The police officer confiscated everything from her car, including her drug box, court date set. No drugs were found in the box, but it was all the paraphernalia. The judge talked to her like it was his daughter, about her life and where it was taking her. He ordered jail or rehab. We checked her into rehab.

Who Are You?

"To Thine Own Self Be True"

I am an Addicts' Mom. Between my daughter on Heroin and my son on Alcohol, my life was a never-ending roller coaster of emotions. Not good emotions, more like anger, fear, helplessness, despair, stress and this uncanny thing called enabling. Shame and embarrassment were normal and I felt that my kids were hopeless, and I sat there watching this drama unfold without any way to help them recover. I was more worried about their lives, than mine. I lost my identity, I was no longer a wife and mother, I was an addicts' mom and felt I would be labeled for life. That was who and what

I was. My dreams and aspirations for myself did not exist, it was not even a question that I could or would succeed in life because my kids would see to it that I was nothing more than their Mother. I was in chains and I would not be set free until I made a decision to take a stand for myself. Aside from all that society says about addicts and their parents, which seems to keep parents at bay with nothing to say or do but to keep their addicted kids at the forefront of their lives. I began to ask myself questions like "Did I cause this?" "What was my responsibility in their addiction?" "Can I change this situation?" Once I started to think differently, is when I started to turn things around for myself and take my life back. I wanted desperately to be whole again. I loved my kids, but I was neglecting the most important aspect of my life, Myself!

I AM, is very powerful, but what does it mean? It means that you are perfect in just the way God created you. How can you not be? You were created to love and be loved. To express and feel joy. When we come from a position of love, anything is possible.

I had to learn this the hard way, I couldn't and wouldn't let go and that was the ego talking. No amount of my suffering or being angry or trying to change things would cure the dis-ease of addiction or anything else for that matter. Why do we have to be in control all of the time? In the 12 Steps Program for Alcoholics Anonymous, it is said to "Let Go and Let GOD". Why are we not able to do this for ourselves for our own sanity? I have discovered, a piece at a time, my power and my life.

In the upcoming Chapters of this book, I will share with you what I did to begin and stay on a healing path. It starts from the inside out. Recovery starts with you! No outward circumstance will ever hope to heal you. I hope to inspire in you the want to take your own journey of healing and taking your life back. I am not fixed completely, but I am in a place of peace now. It will take work, patience and perseverance. At the end of each Chapter, you will find Reflective Questions to ask yourself, Exercises and Affirmations. I ask that you be honest with yourself when writing the answers. The *Affirmations* are there for you to say out loud and to carry around with you, if you so desire, as a reminder of how wonderful and strong you really are. As Parents, especially Mothers, we tend to wear our hearts on our sleeve and every encounter with our kids is a new challenge. I will give keys for success when you feel guilty, angry, helpless, resentful, emotional and lost. I want this for you! I wanted it for me, I just didn't know where to go or who to talk to about ending the insanity. Do this for yourself because you deserve it and you matter!

Reflective Questions

- How do I feel in this moment? Angry? Fearful? Resentful? Happy? Sad?
- What can I do in this moment to change the way I feel? Can I choose peace over turmoil, for just 5 minutes? Can I choose love?
- Do I blame myself for my kids' addiction? Do my kids blame me for their lives? If so, why? Please be honest with this question, because it is the seed that you have planted and must be uprooted.
- Did I raise my kids to be addicts? Now this question might feel a little rhetorical, but it's important for you to answer out loud for the sake of your sanity.
- How have I influenced my kids to handle their lives so recklessly? Again, a question you need to answer out loud. It's frightening that you might think you are responsible.

Exercise—Who Am I?

This is a question that people ponder far too much. Society puts labels on us, especially women that we are *what we do* and we are *what we have*. We are Mothers, Wives, Friends, Sisters and some of us have careers. In our lives at this time, we have another label we are an Addict's Mom. A label we would care to live without, but was dealt this hand of cards and now we must learn to live with it for the rest of our days. Our kids are important to us, we gave birth to them, raised them to be happy confident children, right? When they turned out to be otherwise, we labeled ourselves failures. We questioned ourselves about the choices our kids made and somehow believed that we were responsible for those choices. We took it upon ourselves to be the beast of burden, to cradle them and save them from themselves. We forgot about us and all those other labels became unimportant.

A really powerful exercise is available on my website. It is a "fill in the blank" about who you think you are right now. It will help you get in touch with how you are feeling, what you think about yourself and how you see yourself. I urge you to complete this exercise before moving on to the next chapter. Once you fill in the blanks, put it away and take it out again a year from now. I invite you to download the worksheet and complete the exercise. Download the worksheet at www.sandyLsherman.com/IAMExercise.

Chapter 2

The Three C's

"I didn't cause it.
I can't control it.
I can't cure it"

I was born in 1958, a time when things were simpler, right? Growing up in the 1960's, 1970's and even the 1980's were times where you could actually focus on family. Being a kid meant walking barefoot all summer, swimming, being with friends all day until the sun went down. The TV programs were wholesome and were censored, no swearing, sex and definitely no reality TV. The commercials in the 60's were about cigarettes, Ovaltine, laundry soap, cereal, pickles and aspirin. In the 70's commercials were about Alka Seltzer, Hai Karate Aftershave, Dow Scrubbing Bubbles (which by the way I use!), Folgers Coffee and Mama Mia Spaghetti Sauce. How many licks does it take to get to the end of a tootsie pop? In the 80's you saw Bubble Yum, Pringles, Mrs. Butterworth Syrup, Cocoa Krispies, Barbie's, Nerds and introducing the Nintendo! How about the jingle, I'm a Toys R Us Kid?

Today's TV commercials are about the Top 10, Super Bowl, cars, and the latest and greatest drugs that offer every prescription to treat every ailment we humans have under the sun. From depression, Lipitor, feeling tired, irritable, stressed out, we have a drug for you. Cymbalta, what is that?

Our kids are victims of society, from reality TV to drug commercials that promise us a better life. They show Moms with depression, Dads with erectile dysfunction, you name it, that you can take a drug to cure your ailment. Our children are watching this each and every day and we take it for granted. No wonder it's okay and acceptable. We are raising a generation of kids that thrive on instant gratification, from reality TV to video games to Internet to smart phones. They become numb to it. Now there is nothing wrong with any of that because we all get caught up in it, but what I'm saying is that the drug epidemic is sort of glamorized through what our kids see from a very young age. Society has bred some very savvy kids that seem to know and pick up on all the technology that some of us never had the privilege of learning or knowing. They run circles around us in the tech area. In my State of New Mexico, In 2015, there were 536 people who died from drug overdoses. Prescription opioids, such as hydrocodone and oxycodone, remained the leading cause of overdose deaths; next on the list was Heroin (Morgan Petroski/Albuquerque Journal). More New Mexicans died last year of drug overdoses than in any other year on record. The 536 deaths in 2014 mark a 19 percent increase over the year before, following a two-year decline, according to the state Department of Health. The number shows the state needs to step up efforts to curb addiction, including better monitoring of prescription painkillers, according to state Epidemiologist Dr. Michael Landen. So why am I talking about this?

We, as moms and parents of addicts today, continue to blame ourselves for our kids' choices, even though we had nothing to do with it. Our kids blame us for their lives and their circumstances, family blames us for not being there for our kids, society blames us when our kids become criminals and steal and even kill for their drugs. Here we are trying to raise our families in the millennium and it's more difficult today with all the distractions of the aforementioned and not to mention social media. We are competing with everyone that says it's okay to self-medicate and not face reality.

The Bad Mom Syndrome

When our kids experiment with drugs and turn out to be addicts, we blame ourselves. We become the punching bag for them and everyone else to beat up on us. The Bad Mom Syndrome is one of those ways *we* keep ourselves down and out. It's an out for our kids, an excuse, and an out for society who needs somewhere to place blame, why not us Moms and/or Parents? But, to keep things fair, we as moms do a perfect job of trying to be the "perfect" parent. We compare ourselves to others, which again is not only societal pressure, but also a mindset that we have created. We are insecure about our ability to parent so we try to adapt the next best piece of advice. It causes stress and anxiety that is so unhealthy for our minds and bodies and has an adverse effect on everyone concerned. This is our belief that we don't measure up with the unrealistic idea of being perfect. We play ping-pong with our own standards of raising our kids to be upstanding and productive adults. It's time to relax and be okay with not being okay. What is important is that you love your kids and accept what and who they are in this moment. Don't try to figure them out. Let them figure things out. Being an addicts' mom/parent is painful enough, but blaming yourself for your child's choices of shooting heroin into their veins or drinking a fifth of vodka is your ego talking to you as if you were responsible for making them do it. A contrasting thought would be that one of your kids made the honor roll, was the star football player and received all kinds of awards for being a shining star. My question to you is "Are you responsible for his or her accolades"? Or did your child make a choice to live a happy, motivated, and meaningful life with or without you? It's something to ponder for sure.

she fell
she crashed
she broke
she cried
she crawled

she hurt
she surrendered
and then.......
She rose again
Anonymous

I had such a bad case of Bad Mom Syndrome when my kids were in full swing of their addictions. I contemplated suicide on more than one occasion. It was heart wrenching that I was not good for them or for me. If I was such a bad influence on them then I might as well end it all right here and now. I thought about how I was going to do it, with a boatload of pills and then I would just fall asleep never to awaken. My heart hurt so much I could hardly stand it, I couldn't breathe, and when I spoke with my kids, they would validate my feelings of my own shortcomings with their accusations, foul-mouthed, vulgar speech. They would tell me horrible awful things and although I tried to defend myself, I believed them. Obviously, I never followed through. Why? Because they needed me, my kids needed me. When I thought about them, seeing their faces and hearing their voices, I just couldn't do it. This was not how my story was going to end. I was all they had. I was all I had. I loved them so much and my love would see them through this. I started to turn things around for myself. I started to get stronger by reading and listening to positive daily inspiration. My journey of taking my life back had just begun. I know now it wasn't my fault. It's not your fault either. Bottom line: *you cannot control another only yourself. Remember, and repeat after me, I didn't cause it, I can't control it, and I can't cure it.*

The following Chapters focus on your recovery. The steps necessary to begin your healing are revealed. I've talked about the problem of self- blame, guilt and taking responsibility for your child's choices in the beginning of the book. The rest of this book discusses the solutions and the change you will experience once you take 100% responsibility for your own life and choices and allow your child to do the same. I encourage you to break through the barriers and the walls you have put up, because once you have admitted that change is necessary, you will see a huge transformation and shift in your mindset.

Affirmations for Moms
- I Am Well
- I Am Focused
- I Follow Through

- I Am Calm
- I Am Worthy
- I Am Enough
- I Speak and Think Positively
- My Courage is Stronger Than My Fear
- I Nurture Myself, So I Can Nurture Others
- I Choose to Take Responsibility for My Own Life

Part 2

Create Your Plan
for Recovery

Chapter 3

Recovery Starts with Me

*"I Think That Recovery From Anything Is Honestly
The Most Badass Thing A Person Can Do."*
—Anonymous

When we brought our daughter home from her 5-1/2 month stint at rehab, I knew my healing and recovery had been threatened a bit. It was like we were starting over with her. We had a second chance with our Daughter that was now clean. The poison in her body was no longer. But, the demons remained inside her, calling her with all of their being. She resisted as long as she could, but then it took her mind over again, slowly at first, then with a vengeance that she could not resist. She relapsed 2 months after returning home from recovery. Her Dad and I had taken her phone and had it erased, no familiar numbers on speed dial. She found her way back to the demons that taunted her very being and she abandoned everything she had worked so hard to hold on to, her sobriety. It was subtle at first, but then I felt the familiar pit in my stomach, I began to notice the signs that brought us to this place in time. The numerous bathroom trips that seemed to get longer and longer, the hours of sleeping, 12 to 14 hours at a time, the inability to hold a conversation without falling asleep mid-sentence. Oh My God! I, again, was beside myself and then the old proverbial feeling of denial crept up again. I looked the other way; I didn't want to deal with this shit again. I was appointed the watchdog of our Daughter. I wouldn't let her out of my sight, I took her to work with me, and we joined a gym together where I hired a personal trainer. You can't exercise if you're high, right? Anything and everything I could think of to keep her busy and in my sight. It was exhausting and I wanted to quit this job of my Daughters keeper. She was 19 years old and couldn't be trusted out of my sight. I couldn't micro manage her any longer.

Enough Is Enough

It was the hardest decision in my life to let her go. It was also the best decision in my life to let her go. I began to allow her to make her own decisions, wrong or right.

Allowing the Inevitable

Being in a state of judgment of my kids, or anyone for that matter, was constant. I had my dreams and expectations for them and they were constantly disappointing me. With every phone call came a new drama or disaster in their lives. They liked their drama! They liked their disasters. They liked being miserable and until they changed their thoughts, their lives would remain in a state of turmoil. Like they say the definition of insanity is doing the same thing over and over expecting a different result. When we make a decision not to get caught up in their drama, we can begin to conscientiously move forward.

When I sit down with a Mom with an addicted child, the first thing I explain to her is that her life matters. Together we work on setting up boundaries that she is comfortable with that work for her. We talk about strategies that she can apply immediately and empower her to start to reclaim her life. It begins with letting go.

When Carol came to see me, her life had fallen apart two years prior. She is an author of "The Truth about ADHD" and a very successful Coach on the same topic. She was married, with a Son that had a promising future as an attorney. As her story unfolded, I could feel that she was not over the pain of what occurred. Her Son, who had been accepted to a prestigious college studying law, was a heroin addict. At the time she found out, she felt just as helpless as we all do with addicted kids. Her Son, with a promising future ahead of him, had overdosed in the bathroom of his apartment. His roommate discovered him and made the call to Carol and her husband. She fell apart. She got divorced as the strain of going through the addiction was too much to save the marriage and when their Son died, it was the straw that broke her life. The death of her son and her marriage was all that she could bear. Her practice fell apart, her body fell apart and now 2 years later she felt she was just coming out of her depression. Her son's death took everything out of her. After she finished her story, I asked her if she had let him go. Accepted things as they are and moved forward. To have her own free will, to allow herself to be willing to release her Son and start building her life again, because she mattered. As her coach, I asked her to share with me what had occurred with her Son and the events leading up to this point in time. In order for her to release she had to talk about it, openly and feel the emotions, not repress them. I also encouraged her to set the agenda of our meetings, this wasn't about me fixing her, but about her healing herself by realizing that she was an important part of the healing process. She told me that just by talking about what happened with me she felt a huge weight off of her shoulders. She learned that she could talk about it and detach herself from what occurred. Sometimes we just need to talk about it and get it off our chest. She is in the process of taking her power back and I love that! We continue to talk on a weekly basis and I continue to notice a change in her voice and her energy. She is releasing the guilt and she is striving to nurture herself.

Our healing and recovery starts with us. Our expectations for our children are just that, our expectations. We as Mothers are nurturing and loving and we give our hearts freely even if the recipient is undeserving. It's time to turn that beautiful ingrained ability that we were born with back to ourselves. It's not easy because we fall back into the comfortable position of wanting to save our kids. You might get caught up in their drama, as I did, and the same vicious cycle will be in the forefront of your life. The bad choices my kids made for themselves are no longer an influence in my life. I want this new found freedom to be yours too. Tough Love? Maybe. It's never too late to let your kids take responsibility for their lives, actions, and beliefs. We can allow them to learn for themselves. This was a concept I didn't get for a long time.

Keys to Help You Through When You Are Feeling Weak

Practice relaxation breathing. 10 deep breaths in and out. Breathe all the way down to your abdomen. This signals your body to automatically release the tension.

Meditation. This takes practice. If you could start off for just 10 minutes a day meditating, it will reduce stress, which is so harmful to the body. I have a meditation that you can download *on my website,* www.sandyLsherman.com. This is a Gratitude meditation and it takes just 10 minutes a day. This is a powerful meditation to help you shift your mindset almost immediately.

Listen to something positive daily. Start your morning off with a positive podcast or inspirational audio. This will set your day in the right direction. I find that if I miss a day, it really affects my state of mind.

Read an inspiring book.

Write in a Journal. This is super powerful to write down your thoughts, what you are feeling. I have kept a journal for the past five years, which has really played a huge part in writing this book. I not only wrote what was happening on a given day, but I also wrote sayings, quotes, prayers for my kids and myself. This is part of the healing process.

Don't go it alone. Be with people that inspire and encourage your healing. We need our own tribe that cares about us and believes in us.

Reflective Questions

- What do I uniquely offer to this world? How can I use this to improve my surroundings?

- What am I grateful for today? Write 10 things you are grateful for today in your journal, be sure to date the page! When we are in a state of gratitude, we can appreciate even the smallest of things.

- What do you love about your life today? Please find at least one thing to write down, it will shift your thinking into that of love and appreciation for the beauty that surrounds you.

Exercise

Write a Love Letter to your son or daughter

I encourage you to sit down somewhere quiet, no distractions, and write a love letter to your son or daughter. Let the words flow onto the page and the tears too. This is part of your healing and recovery.

Affirmations

- I release all fears of not being perfect, not good enough
- I release all expectations; I am free to live the life I was meant to live
- I let go of the need to control others
- I allow my kids to make their own decisions
- I will try to live today, in the now, and I will face today head on
- I let go of all of my regrets, that's in the past. Today I will be grateful for the lessons I have learned

Chapter 4

Setting Boundaries

"Today, I will thoughtfully bless and forgive myself"
I will remove "If only" from my vocabulary and I
Will replace these words with
"I did the best I could at the time."
I made the right decision for that moment."
—Nar-Anon SESH Blue Book

When I first saw my son after he was born, he was the most beautiful thing I ever saw. He came into this world just as God created him, perfect in all ways. I was in love with this baby. A mother's love is unconditional for her child for their entire lives. They could do no wrong and you would fight to the death if anyone tried to hurt them.

I remember his personality was one of a happy go lucky kid. He had many friends in school and took an interest in music. He taught himself to play the drums and he became so good at it. I involved him in the kitchen with helping me cook dinner. I remember telling him that I didn't want him to expect a woman to take care of him ever, that he would know how to cook and clean and take care of her. I wanted my Son to be respectful of women and of others and to always have a servant's heart.

Andrew was 16 years old when he left our home. He didn't want to abide by the rules of the household, actually he refused to live by our rules. He was terribly disruptive as a teenager and didn't like school. I was in the principal's office at least once a week to talk about his attitude, his grades and his atrocious absenteeism. He cut so many classes that he would not graduate; he dropped out in the eleventh grade. I eventually had to withdraw him legally so I wouldn't end up in jail. I remember thinking what the hell is he doing? Why doesn't he like school? I know many kids openly admit they don't like school, but my Son was an extreme. When he became an adult, he confessed he felt bored and also felt he knew more than the instructors did. I thought that was his ego talking. Come to find out, my son has a genius IQ. So if he's so smart, why does he drink? Why can't he hold a job longer than 3 months? Why is he not taking responsibility for his choices?

I never knew he had a problem until about 6 years ago. Andrew is 29 years old, lives in Portland, Oregon, with his Fiancé and his two beautiful sons. When he's sober, he is the most sensitive and beautiful person. We are so connected sometimes; I love that side of him. He pursued his love for cooking and, when he can hold a job, he is a Soux Chef and a brilliant one at that. Being a chef is his calling; he is also a vegan. When he drinks, he turns into this monster. Drinking continues to give him excuses to not keep a job, take responsibility for his own life. He escapes from feeling anything. After admitting that he is an alcoholic, he feels that being inconsiderate and vile to the people he loves is just a side effect. It's the booze talking. And that's okay? Nope! Not anymore. We would get caught up in these conversations where he would throw all the blame, all the responsibility and all his anger at me. I would be caught off guard sometimes and get sucked up in his little horror movie. Being my Son, I do love him very much and I'm very proud of him when he's sober. He's been in and out of detox centers for the past 6 years. So the line I had to draw with him was "I'll only talk to you when you are sober". Case closed. It can't be any other way.

My kids have taught me valuable lessons. They taught me to change my thoughts and it changed my life. It's still a healing journey, but I've got it handled and I know what to say and do. It's amazing how I feel most days now. I have given myself permission to be happy!

Unconditional Love is caring about the happiness of another person without any thought for what we might get for ourselves. As a mother of two addicts, I find this definition to be not so true. I love my kids and always had put them before myself. There was a time before the addictions where I would have agreed. My own mother always told me that my sister and I always came first before her needs. Her needs were met after we were in bed at night when she could finally take a breather from the day. In the middle of the addiction, I put my kids first, their needs came before mine and around midnight when the house was quiet, I was in quiet despair. My kids were silently killing me little by little. But, by now, I was learning to take care of myself at an alarming rate. I was setting boundaries, drawing the line in the sand

and treating myself with the respect and love I deserved. I would not give in to their every whim and was on guard constantly so I could pounce if they tried to manipulate me. The unconditional love now had a few conditions. I did care about their happiness, but I would not be manipulated or harassed for something that they wanted, mainly drugs and to stay high as long as possible. They no longer monopolized the conversation whether it was in person or on the phone. I would simply hang up if the conversation was not a positive one for me. I have always been there when they were ready to ask for help, but I would no longer be a victim or a punching bag or at their mercy.

My Way or the "High" Way

When I made the decision to let my kids go and take my life back, I had drawn the line and set the boundary of "You will NOT do drugs in my house ever again and you will NOT come to my house high." There is no negotiation in this scenario. It's my life that I'm protecting now and I will not watch them kill themselves in front of me. I know that sounds harsh, maybe even a little bit unfeeling. Until you take a stand right now, you will not be free. Set yourself free of the blame and responsibility. Set yourself free of being a victim.

Give some unconditional love to yourself. Set yourself free of having to witness them in a state of euphoria, a drunken stupor. You deserve better than this. Yes, it is a dis-ease. Until you heal and become strong enough to handle your life, you cannot handle theirs.

When Linda came to see me her son was still living with her. Her son, David, was 42 years old and an alcoholic. Her son relied on her to take care of him and really had no ambition or motivation to have a life of his own. He felt that she was still responsible and made no attempts to leave. She felt guilty and responsible for his happiness and enabled him by allowing him to continue to live there with no job, sucking her energy dry, as well as providing him with money, a car, a reason to abuse her mentally. She was caught up in the guilt that if she asked him to leave, he would have nowhere to go. We began to build a plan on setting boundaries for her to implement immediately. In our session, together we talked about a workable solution, first of all, setting a date for her son to leave, ready or not. She got excited at the possibility of living alone; it gave her a sense of peace. Setting a date was the first step in reclaiming her life. The second step was knowing that her letting go of her adult son was not giving up on him, but realizing that the responsibility for his own life started with him and not her. Once she started to shift her thinking, her transformation had begun. Her life was important and she mattered. By admitting to herself that she enabled him, she was able to take action steps toward shifting the responsibility from herself to her son without the guilt and anger she felt in the past. Her recovery had begun.

Forgiveness

To set boundaries we have to learn to forgive our children and ourselves. The healing you will and are experiencing comes in many forms. It does not come from any outside source, but comes from inside of you. I have asked for many miracles in my journey of healing and feel that so many times they have happened. It started with forgiveness. Forgiveness for myself. Forgiveness for my kids for treating me and everyone they cared about with such unacceptable behavior. When I started to forgive, I started to feel inner peace. I was releasing the resentment and the anger and the fear. *A Course in Miracles* says, our greatest tool for changing the world is our capacity to 'change our mind about the world'. So, "change your thoughts, change your life" is a mantra I live by. Love is the only real thing in life, everything else is just an illusion. When you start to believe in yourself and surround yourself with people that believe in you, you can accomplish anything. Anything in life is possible! I love this thought and I think of it often. It is possible for you to be happy! It is possible for your kids to get and stay clean. It is possible for you to feel peace, feel joy, feel and be happy! It's a choice! It's all a choice. The terrifying part of recognizing that you have the power to change your life is not the fear of 'can I do it?' but Oh My God, now I am responsible for my life. But, you are the creator of your life, are you not? What an awesome thought! You CAN rewrite your story, starting now. You can begin now. How will your story end? I talk with my clients all the time about their stories and breaking thru the barriers that hold them in a constant continuum of feeling stuck. Remember Linda's story? She was stuck in a life with her adult alcoholic Son, his problems, his drama, his entitlement. Until she started to change her thoughts and started to set boundaries and shift the responsibility of her Son's life back to him, where it belonged. She began to live an empowered life. She had let him go to make his own choices. It's awesome when you have a breakthrough and realize that when you start to forgive yourself for your child's addiction you release your need to take the blame or the responsibility for their choices.

Keys For Keeping Your Sanity

- Don't feel bad for locking up your stuff! Put deadbolts on your bedroom and your closets and keep your valuables locked up!

- Don't give them money! If they are hungry, do buy them food. If they need gas, fill their tank. If you give them money it will go straight to their dealer for drugs. If your kids are in recovery, still, do not give them money!

- Don't rescue them when they get themselves into a jam or get arrested. I made this mistake and bailed my Son out of jail, paid for a high priced attorney and got him on probation only for him to continue his addiction. They have no conscience or any regard for you!

- Do get yourself into a support group, whether it be Al-Anon or Nar-anon or a Church group. Surround yourself with like-minded people to inspire and motivate you to take care of yourself. This is awesome therapy!

- Do take the time to educate yourself and research the addiction and stay informed so you know what you are dealing with.

- Do try and attempt to get them into rehab. I know that it is their ultimate choice if they are an adult and you cannot force them to go. Financially, there are several programs out there that will fit your budget if not covered by insurance. I have listed some of these facilities in the Valuable Resources in the back of this book.

Reflective Questions/Exercise

- Do you remember what you did and how you felt prior to your child's addiction? Write it down. Were you happy, content, satisfied with your life? I want you to remember a time in your life when you were the happiest and write that story.
- Write a letter to someone that you might have not forgiven in your life. Write exactly what is on your mind, all the resentment, anger, everything. Then I want you to burn this letter and release it. Let It Go!
- Have you forgiven yourself?

Chapter 5

Reclaim Your Power

"I discovered I always have choices and
sometimes it's only a choice of attitude."
—Judith Knowlton

What does the phrase "Reclaim Your Power" mean? Why is it so important to reclaim your life when you are dealing with an addicted child? Is it selfish to want to feel a sense of peace or a shred of happiness? We keep hundreds of agreements with all kinds of sources, people, family, friends, career, etc., but the most important agreement we need to keep is with ourselves. This agreement is to live our life with dignity and self-respect. All we want is to have our kids be sober, clean and live a life that we have imagined for them. That is our dream come true and most parents take this for granted when their child grows up and moves on without becoming drug addicted or alcohol induced. It's not even a thought and why should it be? A normal family, with normal kids is not in our vocabulary. That's why you are here reading this book. You are searching for answers and solutions and you just want to feel normal again, to feel something other than worry, guilt, rage and being helpless. To reclaim your power over yourself is a process and a personal journey that you are going through right now. This Chapter is about taking your life back. It's about the incredible power you have within yourself to make that happen. It's about believing in yourself and having the self-confidence to change. Are you ready to make that change? The following steps will put you on a path to reclaiming your power.

Stop Enabling Addiction

Are you loving someone to death? This is a question that we as parents often wonder about. The more we do, the more they want. It is what we resolve to do to rescue them from the clutches of their substance abuse. We save our kids only to find out that one, they don't remember and two they don't care. The only time they reach out is when they need money, otherwise we don't hear from them for months. I always knew when I was enabling my kids. There was always this pit in my stomach and my intuition was screaming at me loud and clear that what I was about to give them was not the right thing to do. You have everything to lose and nothing to gain from enabling your addicted kid. The following comparison is what I came up with to determine the difference between enabling vs. helping:

YOU ENABLE THEM BY:

- **Giving Money When Asked**—They will beg, plead, cry, yell, threaten. They will say things like, "I am starving, I need gas money, I have a doctor's appointment and I need the co-pay, (this was my daughter's favorite), or I have to pick up my prescription." Be aware that the ONLY thing they need money for is to support their habit and buy more drugs.

- **Paying for A Car**—A car, gas, insurance, etc., is needed to go to work or school, they are also using it to meet their dealer, go to the pawn shop, and transport drugs to other addicts. They also use this car to transport everything they have stolen from you.

- **Paying for a Phone**—You want to stay in touch with them so you pay for their phone, I get it, I did pay for my daughter's phone. However, remember, that they buy their drugs using this phone and have their dealers on speed dial.

- **Paying for or Providing a Place to Live**—Either she is living in your home, or you are providing money to pay rent, utilities, or even spring for a hotel room. You are providing a place for her to get high, and you are also providing a place for her to overdose in your bathroom or in another strange place. Let them find their own shelter to use. You don't want to watch her kill herself.

- **Bailing Them Out of Jail**—Bailing him out of jail and bringing him home only continues to contribute and condones the drug abuse. Help him by not bailing him out of jail.

You Love Them By:
- **Giving Them Food**—Taking them out to eat and buying her a meal is a way to stay in contact and also

allows you to open up a conversation on whether she is ready to get help. It provides the opportunity to offer help.

- **Seeking Professional Help**—Contacting an interventionist. A professional interventionist can open up communication with your son, along with family involvement, and increases the chances for him to enter treatment. This is an option for some, not all. I have seen this work and I have seen this backfire where a kid absolutely refuses to move forward. Remember, some addicts like being addicts. You have to know your own child before hiring an interventionist.

- **Getting Treatment**—She needs it. If she had cancer, you would do anything to get her medical treatment and help her put the disease into remission. Getting her into rehab is putting her drug addiction into remission. Let me preface this statement. Rehab treatment programs are not a guarantee that the addict will not relapse when they return, it's possible and likely. This is not for every addicted kid and you shelling out thousands of dollars may not be the right choice for your family.

- **Answering the Phone**—Always try and answer the phone, but stay strong. You can tell him how much you love him and always ask the question "Are you ready to go into treatment" or "Are you ready to get help" If he's not ready then let go until he comes to you for help.

- **Treating The Disease Like the Disease It Is**—As I mentioned in a previous Chapter, drug addiction is a disease and educating yourself about the specific drug of choice will arm you with the signs and symptoms which will increase your chances of getting them into the right treatment program that will treat the disease for life, not just a temporary fix. Again, you know your child so if your child is not ready, willing and able, there is nothing you can do.

When I talk with my clients I advise them that enabling their son or daughter is a vicious cycle that never ends up in their favor. If they continue to give them money, for instance, their kids will go to extremes to get the money from them. I remember my daughter tracked me down while I was running errands one day. She was in the parking lot standing next to my car when I came out. She proceeded to ask me for $88 for a prescription she had to pick up that day. Now, $88 is a really odd number, but she was exact. I refused and she stood in front of my car and said if I didn't give her the money, she wouldn't move from the front of my car. She got hysterical and more demanding. I would have to run her over and that seemed fine with her at the time. She wasn't budging. She was about to choose dying over stepping out of the way to get that $88. Needless to say, I did not give her the money, but it was a standoff of more than an hour. She finally left. If we, as parents, continue to be victimized, manipulated and bullied by our addicted kids, currently or in the past, let me ask you this: Who is allowing this to happen or continue?

There Is Nothing Left For You to Do

I mentioned in a previous chapter that letting go was the best thing I could have done for my life. Many parents become spiritual when their kids are addicts, mainly because we want to feel something other than the pity for our addicted kids. Once I admitted and accepted that I was powerless and started to turn my mindset around, I was starting to free myself of the chains that bound me. We can ultimately thank our children for being such awesome teachers. It teaches us to let go of all the anger, fear, helplessness, despair that we have been feeling for far too long. It's an emancipation, so to speak, that we can let our kids go and find that we are going to be more than okay. It's a freedom that I sought after for many years and have finally found the peace I was looking for. We do not have to be slaves to our children's addictions. We can let go of our need to rescue them, take care of them, pity them or enable them.

The Power of Animals

The love of an animal and the love you have for an animal is an extremely powerful force of nature. I truly believe that animals have super powers to help heal grief and give back without speaking a word. The trust that animals give us with no expectation of returned affection is what gives us hope to keep moving forward. My own animals, namely my horses and dogs, were always there when I needed them. Being in their presence was healing for me. They took my mind off the reality that was currently unfolding. Whether you saddle up or grab a leash, having them with you in your time of need always is a true blessing. Being with God's creatures is soothing and makes the situation somehow bearable, at least for the time we spend with our animals. We learn to develop compassion for ourselves and others. If you have animals in your life, take some time to be with them and experience their joy and happiness. Take a walk in nature with your favorite dog or horse, play with your cat on the floor, sing to your bird. You will find the power of their presence helps you feel more grounded, might even make you laugh and feel joy. Life is still waiting for you. Go embrace it!

The Power of Positivity

The power of being positive is a conscious choice. Being positive does not mean you have to fake it if you are angry or things aren't going your way, it's more of a mindset to choose joy and peace over anger and fear. You are being defeated by your child's addiction; you are struggling to get through the day sometimes. I am not making light of how you are feeling when you have an addicted kid, but I am pointing out that you permit the situation to control your mind and dominate your life. Being and staying positive through the hell you are living through takes work and perseverance, but it is the essence of a peaceful mind. We sometimes look outside of ourselves to gain positivity and make us feel better. The answer, though, is on the inside of us. To help you with this positive thing, I want you to take out a sheet of paper and write down the values that are most important to you. For example, your husband who loves you, your kids that you love, your integrity; always doing the right thing and the best you can, your job, your health, etc. Write what each value means to you. This is kind of a gratitude list, the difference is that the list is coming from inside of you and what's important to you right now. It's your assets list. Your values are who you are. Fill your mind with thoughts of faith and confidence and security. What this does is get rid of thoughts of doubt, anger, lack of faith, insecurities and fears.

Emotional Scale

Being in touch with how we are feeling and why is the beginning in recognizing when we are resisting and pushing against what we are supposed to be feeling. It's the beginning of your healing. You are on a roller coaster ride with your kids and your emotions. I was in a state of hurt most of the time and when I got angry, it seemed to make me feel better like I could conquer the demons inside me. I could stand up for myself and take a stand for my well-being. I knew that my anger would subside after a short time. I wanted to feel joy and love and I did make it to that point after much practice. The slightest improvement is so great. You become aware of where you are and where you want to be. Try this exercise; List all your emotions that you could possibly feel. Put a checkmark next to the ones you are currently feeling. Ask yourself why you are feeling this way. Then, ask yourself how you could move up or down on the emotional scale. What is an emotional scale? Think of it like a gauge where the needle goes from right to left or up to down. It's what and how we are feeling in any given moment. You could be high on the scale and feel joy, empowerment, freedom, love and passion or you could be low on the scale and feel fear, depression, despair, helplessness. In between there is doubt, worry, blame, anger, discouragement, hatred, rage. If you are feeling fear, how can you feel a little safety? If you are feeling optimistic, how can you feel positive expectation and so on. You can download my version of the emotional scale on my website, www.sandyLsherman.com/EmotionalScale (Interpreted from Esther and Jerry Hicks, The Teachings of Abraham)

The Power of Your Dreams

When was the last time you thought about your dreams? Did you lose track of your own hopes and aspirations? What about before the addicted child surfaced? What were you doing with your life? Were you just living day to day with no plans or were you actually working toward something that would make you happy? When all of this hit the fan, you probably put yourself last as you were scrambling with your confusion and powerlessness. I ask my clients to tell me what their vision is starting in a year from now. I want them to describe what their life looks like in 12 months. What does your life look like? What are your goals? The goals I want them to describe is in 4 categories; Personal goals, professional goals, health goals, and financial goals. I ask the question over and over again. What I'm truly looking for is "What does your life look like for you outside of dealing with the addiction of your kids?" It's a beautiful thing to listen to them focus on themselves and actually getting a little excited about taking their life and giving it meaning. This is a great exercise. If you could wave a realistic magic wand, what would your life look like a year from now? What would you do if you had complete freedom? Grab a piece of paper and write down your vision of your dream life. I'm hoping that you will do this exercise with an open heart and open eyes. I would love to hear your dream story. Share it with me at sandysherman57@gmail.com.

The Power of Self-Love

I think every personal development book I have ever read says something about loving ourselves. I heard someone say "If you tell me to love myself one more time, I'm going to slap you". Well, you may laugh and agree with this statement, but in order to heal, you have to make some effort to love yourself. What this means is to pay attention and be aware of your self-talk. You are harder on yourself than anyone around you could be. You tell yourself you are a bad parent, you hate your body, you are ugly, you don't know what you are doing, you don't like your hair and on and on. You would not talk to someone you love and care about in this manner, why do you talk to yourself like that? If you could tell yourself something positive about yourself, what would that be? You can say as many awesome things about yourself as you want. If you feel awkward, tell yourself in private or just think it, but it's necessary. You can tell yourself things like: "I'm a great listener", "I have a pretty smile", "I have a great sense of humor", "I'm a compassionate person", etc. or anything else you can think of. Give it a try and whenever you are thinking negatively about yourself, please try and replace it with positive reinforcement.

Gratitude

When we are in a stuck moment, it's hard to see positive forces when challenges and obstacles are blaring and fears are looming. This is a great time to be grateful. Not grateful for what has us stuck, but appreciating and seeing what doesn't. Gratitude helps us see our situation in a way that can lessen panic and open up our thinking to new solutions. Gratitude is "The Elixir of Life"

I have so much to be grateful for in my life and I say "thank you" every morning when I get out of bed. I believe that life is a gift and not a right and I want to live my life in a constant state of appreciation and gratitude. I am alive and I am well and everything in my world is beautiful. Gratitude brings abundance. If you are grateful, you bring about much more to be grateful for.

When we see the good, as well as, the bad, it becomes more difficult to complain and stay stuck. The awareness of what we're grateful for can bring us happiness almost in an instant. If we can practice gratitude on a daily basis, even for the smallest things, then we can realize that our life, our relationships, our peace, improves our health, our outlook on life, reduces stress and basically makes us a happier person. As I mentioned in a preceding Chapter, writing in your journal every day is therapeutic. Write what you're grateful for, even if it's just the fact you showered today. When you put yourself in the mindset of gratitude, pretty soon you are listing 10 or 20 things you find yourself being thankful for. It's a great ritual. It will also put you in a state of peace. That's what we are looking for ultimately. This is another powerful tool I use in my Coaching. It puts you in a state of mind of being thankful for your life. I want to suggest that you go out and buy one of the best journals you can find, along with a really nice pen to write with. You will be amazed how it makes you feel when you open it up to write in it. It will truly make you smile.

It's a Matter of Health

When my daughter came home from rehab, I tried to keep her as busy as possible. There was no manual sent home with her for parents on what to do when they come home or get out of rehab. We were on our own trying to recreate the structure she had while living in rehab. I was at a loss so I took her one Sunday to our nearest gym to join. I always thought that exercise was an integral part of recovery. The benefit of working out will help heal the body and the brain. It releases serotonin and the dopamine gland is stimulated as it returns to normal after being chemically induced for so long. It was a great step in getting her to commit to 3 times per week to work out for 1 hour. What it ended up doing was helping me with my recovery, as well. Keeping that commitment for me was improving my mental health and mood. You don't have to be a fitness nut or guru, any daily or weekly physical activity can help strengthen your heart muscle, lower your blood pressure, control your cholesterol, improve blood flow, etc. I encourage my clients to get some form of exercise in daily, whether it's walking, jogging, biking or going to the gym, it's necessary to release those endorphins and alleviate stress. Get up and move your body. You deserve it!

The Power of Partnership

Parents are under tremendous pressure with an addicted child. From a mother's perspective, I always enabled my daughter, where my husband had developed the complete opposite perception. I would give her everything she wanted and asked for and he wanted her to suffer for her consequences. Remember Carol's Story, where the pressures of her addicted son were too much to withstand keeping her marriage together. She enabled her son, while he blamed her for her weakness. In these difficult situations we tend to strike out at each other, when we should be pulling together a united front. It doesn't always work out that way. In her case, she lost her husband and her son. She had lost everything that mattered to her in life. Nothing is resolved when you are at each other's throats and blaming each other and expecting each other to view the situation in their eyes. It doesn't work. What does work is pulling together and becoming a dynamic duo. I can honestly tell you from my own experience that our daughter plays one against the other, she doesn't care who wins, or if you stay together, she only cares about keeping you both at odds and the weaker one she will attack with a vengeance. This is so manipulative and she felt if we were both battling that she had more opportunity to continue the substance abuse. My husband and I survived and we are stronger than ever. Unfortunately, many parents end up ending their marriage because it's just too much for them to handle and they have split views and emotions that no longer will hold them together. I have many clients where this is happening right now and has happened, as in Carol's Story. Don't let this happen to you. I can help you join together and work together as a team, so to speak, to hold and build your united front. It's necessary otherwise you just might lose what's most important to you. You can draw the line where your child cannot penetrate and stay strong to save your partnership. You don't have to see eye to eye and you can have differing opinions, you are only human, but to be on a level playing field, each contributing their own strengths without allowing their child to ruin the union between them.

I encourage my parents to be proactive rather than reactive. It's a sad situation when I see a relationship fall apart because the parents have allowed their addicted kids to destroy them. It's so important to reclaim your power and now you have the tools to begin to do so.

Affirmations

- I Believe in Myself Today
- My Dreams Are Important and I Will Visualize My Dreams Today
- I Will Talk to Myself with Love and Respect Today
- I Have Courage and Strength Today to Get Through Anything
- My Animals Will Help Me with My Healing Today
- I Deserve a Walk in Nature Today

Chapter 6

Foundation to Rebuild

"No one saves us but ourselves.
No one can say and no one may.
We ourselves must walk the path"
—Buddha

The Serenity Prayer, Redefined
God, grant me the serenity to accept
The people I can't change, the courage to change
the one I can, and the wisdom to know it's me

A Broadened Understanding—
On the Road to The Recovery of You

Throughout this book, I have given you powerful questions to ask yourself and we have touched on the innercises that will help you discover who you are in this scenario of your drug and alcohol addicted child. I have also laid out the fact that you did not cause your child's addiction and their choices were their decisions and their decisions alone. On this road of your recovery, I want you to feel empowered and positively keep moving forward. There will be set backs and challenges always, even in a normal life. We all have these crop up from time to time. In the world of drug addiction, we continue to feel isolated from the normal world. What I share with my clients is when you do have a setback or a challenge that arises that you think you can't handle, I want you to remember to ask yourself, when you feel weak, the questions throughout this book. Questions like "Did I cause my child to become an addict"? "Am I responsible for my kid's choices"? "What can I do, in this moment, to change the way I feel?" The answer is most likely No and you can change the way you feel at any given moment just by changing your thoughts.

What About The Buttinski's?

> *"When you judge others, you do not
> define them, you define yourself"*
> —Dr. Wayne Dyer

I had to deal with people trying to give me advice on how to deal with my daughter. I just wanted to touch base on this subject because I know it comes up for you. You think you know people, but in fact you find out how they really feel when you have drug or alcohol-addicted children. The advice and comments and judgment that come out of their mouths really astounded me. The advice seems to run rampant among family, friends, co-workers and you just sit there and listen. My advice to you about people that seem to know everything about dealing with addicted kids is save your energy and your breath! They mean well and feel they are just trying to help. Just say thank you and advise them that if you need their help, you will call them.

Stay strong. I want you to reclaim your power at that very moment you are having challenges, but, and this is a big but, I do want you to feel the feelings such as anger, frustration, powerlessness and fear because you have to feel them completely to let them go. Do not repress your feelings. I am with you and I believe in you. Believe in yourself and claim that individual inside of you that is so beautiful and unique.

5 Short Chapters—A story of taking your life back

Chapter 1
I walk down the street.
There is a deep hole in the sidewalk.
I fall in.
I am lost…I am hopeless.
It isn't my fault.
It takes forever to find a way out.

Chapter 2
I walk down the same street.
There is a deep hole in the sidewalk.
I pretend I don't see it.
I fall in again.
I can't believe I am in this same place
But it isn't my fault.
It still takes a long time to get out.

Chapter 3

I walk down the same street.

There is a deep hole in the sidewalk.

I see it there.

I still fall in...it's a habit...but,

My eyes are open

I know where I am.

It is my fault.

I get out immediately.

Chapter 4

I walk down the same street.

There is a deep hole in the sidewalk.

I walk around it.

Chapter 5

I walk down another street.

—Portia Nelson

I love this story, for me this was my life for so many years until I took the step to go a different direction. I went down a different street. I did not regress, I did not go backwards; I went forward and took responsibility for my life, for my decisions. A positive direction to heal, to take my life back and reclaim my power over my circumstances. Before that,

I blamed outside distractions and myself for everything that was happening to me. I had to take responsibility for my life and my decisions, which included letting my kids go. I was not entitled to a different life, a life to be happy, a life of true bliss. There was only one person responsible for the quality of my life, Me. I had to give up all the excuses I was telling myself: that I was a victim and I was helpless, my lack of awareness and fear was holding me back. Sometimes it's hard to admit that you have the power for everything that does or doesn't happen to you. It's a choice too. Choose wisely. You definitely will not regret it.

All my clients are my favorite clients, my favorite people. I love them all, each and every one of them. Their stories are unique, but still, hauntingly familiar to me. When I met with Kathy, she told me she was ready to make a change in her life. She was taking care of her adult son who was an alcoholic and less than ambitious. She was ready to let him go. He was in and out of recovery programs and detox centers during the last 10 years. As I described in the previous chapters, she had gone through the same pain that we all have experienced. The stealing, lying, cheating, violence, manipulation, and most of all, bashing with vial language, making her the victim and blaming her for his circumstance.

My clients all have similar and familiar stories. Kathy had a little different story at the end though. She told me her son was clean and sober and in recovery for almost 6 months. But the manipulation and the attitude of entitlement continued. A little different perspective because she wanted him to be a normal, upstanding, self-reliant young man, so much so, that she continued to help him with whatever he wanted. Although he wasn't drinking any longer, it seems that he hadn't grown up, he still acted like he was a kid. It was almost 10 years of drinking and it seemed that he had lost his childhood. Kathy told me that things were not better and she was, again, at her wits end. She didn't know what to do at this point. Her son was 25 years old and still living at home with no job and no motivation to get one. He slept till noon every single day, he would stagger out of his room to eat something and then watch TV and play video games all afternoon. I told her that most drug addicts still have the tendency to keep their past behaviors because, quite frankly, it worked! They just have a smile on their face and promises in their heart and you are running for your wallet to help them out. So, let's change this scenario, I told her. First of all, we need to get you in a mindset of strength and courage. What I mean by that, is that you have to become the mother again and him the child. What makes this so great is that he's an adult and being an adult, can make adult decisions and take full responsibility for his own life. Yay! I know it's not a cause for celebration, but it's a step in the right direction. So, as I outlined a strategy for her, we discussed what would work and what wouldn't, after all she had to be 100% on board. The both of us brainstormed a strategy and set boundaries and came up with an action plan. She was terrified as if she was dealing with a complete stranger, except this was her son. To sum it up, he had to leave and she had to take her life back. She set a date for him to be out. This was not easy for her, but she knew she had to take this step. She gathered up friends as advocates on the day he was to be out and they all gave her permission to call them if he resisted. They gave her complete support and would be there to make sure her plan was carried out and she was protected. Kathy gave her son plenty of time to vacate; she advised him to get a job because after D-Day, he was no longer her responsibility. She left him alone after the conversation, allowing it to sink in. She had every intention of following through with her decision and she felt a huge relief and a sense of peace to finally take action. The strategies and action plan we put together for her started with letting go of her son and asking him to leave and after he was gone she would only allow him visitation on her terms. For the next several weeks, he tried to come back, call her for money, for gas, for food, for anything he could. She stayed strong and determined. She had to reclaim her life and she did just that. This whole ordeal was hard for her, after all, she loved him with all of her heart. I was so proud of her.

Affirmations

- I am courageous and I stand up for myself
- I acknowledge my own self-worth and my confidence is soaring
- I am at peace with all that has happened because I know I can handle today
- My life is just beginning
- I draw from my inner strength and light
- I trust myself
- I focus on breathing and grounding myself
- I will allow myself to be happy

Conclusion

I have heard so many times that things happen for a reason, not sure if that is entirely true, but I do know that my life never made a lot of sense until now. I was put here to share my message with you all. I was put on this earth to raise addicted children, believe it or not, because my kids gave my life meaning and something to fight for. They have been my greatest teachers and I wouldn't trade my life for anything on earth. I want you to feel that you matter and you deserve a life of meaning. I want you to take your life back that is my wish for you. Your dream come true is to have your kids clean and sober and for some of you, this will happen. For some of you, it will not. But, in our quest for answers, we must know our path to be happy and at peace. I know now what my life was directed to do, looking back and discovering myself. I took my life back and I am at peace and the happiest I've ever been. This journey does not end here, I will continue my personal journey of my own development and I will help as many as I can to do the same.

I'm so happy to announce that my kids are clean and sober and off drugs and alcohol. They are on their own making their choices and dealing with life's challenges. I'm very proud of how far they have come and I love them with all my heart.

Thank you for reading my book. My ultimate wish is that you continue your journey of healing and recovery and your quest for peace and happiness and know that it is all in your hands. I hope my book has helped you and given you the tools and keys to take your life back and find that positive change to take you farther.

Acknowledgements

First, my sincere thanks and love for my kids, Andrew and Alexis, for having and keeping an open mind through my whole book writing process. Without you, this book would not have been written.

Writing a book was something I always knew I would do, someday! Bringing it to life is another thing. Thank you to all of you that gave me encouragement, feedback, love, and the inspiration to make my dream come true.

To Angela Lauria at The Difference Press who gave me incredible feedback, encouragement and the vision to write this book. Thank you for keeping me accountable and believing in me enough to be so transparent, honest, and so helpful to get it done in 9 weeks. Thank you for acknowledging me as an Author and for publishing my book. This has been an incredible and wondrous journey, which I feel is just the beginning. Love You!

To Women In New Recovery (WINR), thank you for taking my daughter and showing her and giving her a sober life. Your center does amazing work with women that are addicted to drugs and alcohol. I will never forget the counselors that shaped my daughter and gave her a second chance. You helped in saving her life.

To all the Mom's out there with addicted children! Thank you for being Mom's and facing this terrible epidemic. I applaud you for being so brave and not giving up the fight. Thank you for finding value in this book. My hopes and dreams for this book is to help you live a more positive life and continue your healing, always.

To JB Glossinger at Morningcoach.com Thank you for being there for me every single morning, in your Podcast, and never leaving me in my deepest darkest hours. You were an inspiration and gave me the permission to find value in my life, forgive myself and believe in myself. I became motivated to live a life that mattered and finally share my message with the world in this book.

To all my spiritual teachers that helped heal my heart and my mind, Wayne Dyer, Gabrielle Bernstein, Brendon Burchard, Jack Canfield, Les Brown, Mastin Kipp. You taught me so much and I'm forever grateful.

To the Morgan James Publishing team: Special thanks to David Hancock, CEO & Founder for believing in me and my message. To my Managing Editor, Margo Toulouse, thanks for making the process seamless and easy. Many more thanks to everyone else, but especially Jim Howard, Bethany Marshall, and Nickcole Watkins.

About the Author

 Sandy Sherman is an author, an entrepreneur and a parent recovery coach. She focuses on helping moms of drug and alcohol addicted kids because she's lived it herself. Through her coaching program, she has developed powerful techniques for parents to learn how to tend to their own needs so they are best able to help not only their children but also themselves through recovery.

Sandy lives in New Mexico with her wonderful husband, two beautiful horses, a crazy and awesome English Springer Spaniel named Merlin, and a Pit-Bull "our little piglet" named Kita.

Thank You

Thank you for reading this book. The fact that you have gotten to the end and are reading this now tells me that you are ready to positively change and make a shift in your life that truly matters. You're ready to take your life back and I'm so proud of you!

I would love to continue to support your journey in life. I have created a Toolkit of Self-Care Practices for Your Mind, Body & Soul. This is a token of my gratitude. Please accept it as my free gift. Please visit my website www.sandyLsherman. com/Toolkitforselfcare to download your toolkit. In the toolkit, you will find tips and keys to help you stay on your path of healing. Taking care of yourself is crucial, even amidst crisis. It is crucial that you continue your journey in taking your life back and your path to recovery.

I would love to hear from you. Please send me an email with your comments, questions, suggestions or for a free coaching consultation, email sandysherman57@gmail.com Your life does matter and I believe in you!

Please connect with me on Facebook—https://www.facebook.com/SandyLSherman/

I invite you to join my Group Page on Facebook—Mom's In New Recovery—https://www.facebook.com/groups/860930524047980/

Website: www.SandyLSherman.com

Valuable Resources: www.SandyLSherman.com/ValuableResources

Morgan James
Speakers Group

www.TheMorganJamesSpeakersGroup.com

We connect Morgan James published
authors with live and online events
and audiences whom will benefit
from their expertise.

CPSIA information can be obtained
at www.ICGtesting.com
Printed in the USA
LVOW11s1052110318
569445LV00002B/367/P